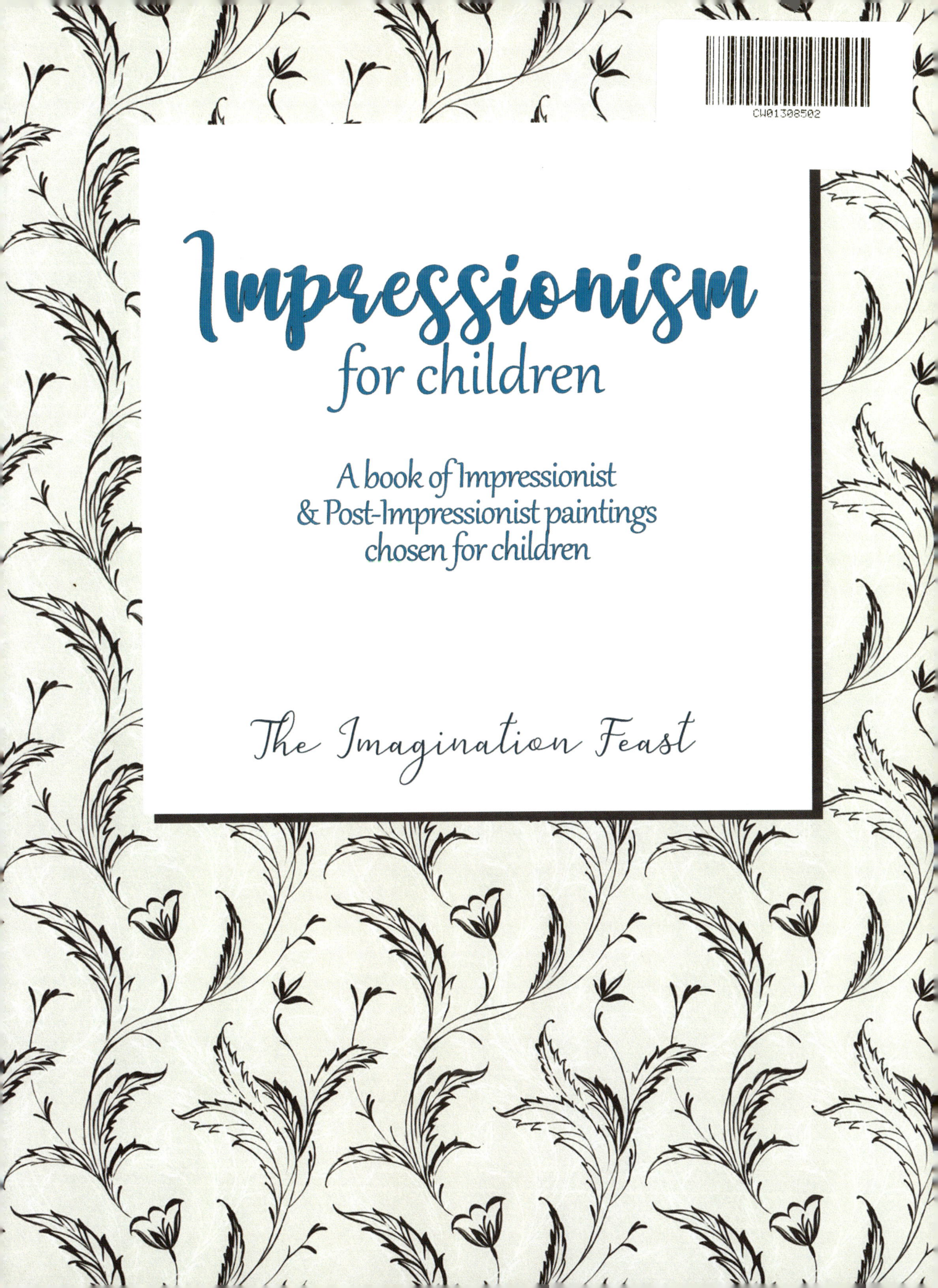

Impressionism
for children

A book of Impressionist
& Post-Impressionist paintings
chosen for children

The Imagination Feast

The Imagination Feast

© The Imagination Feast, 2021, All Rights Reserved

Impressionism
for children

"When you go out to paint, try to forget what objects you have before you, a tree, a house, a field or whatever. Merely think here is a little square of blue, here an oblong of pink, here a streak of yellow, and paint it just as it looks to you, the exact colour and shape, until it gives your own naïve impression of the scene before you."

Claude Monet's advice to Lilla Cabot Perry

The Impressionist artists developed their style of painting in the 19th century. Using relaxed brush strokes and vibrant colours, they created an impression of the scene before them. They loved to paint outdoors in the natural light. They thought carefully about the shapes and the colours they observed.

After this time, some painters developed a style with even bolder colours and more abstract shapes. This was called 'Post-Impressionism'. Vincent van Gogh is, perhaps, the most famous Post-Impressionist artist.

In this volume, the two styles are put together simply as a feast of beautiful art for young children. So much of the work of Impressionism and Post-Impressionism resonates with the observations and wonder of childhood: the way the light falls, the vivid colours, ordinary moments of family love and the everyday scenes of work and play.

'Woman with a Parasol Madame Monet and Her Son,'

Claude Monet, 1875

National Gallery of Art

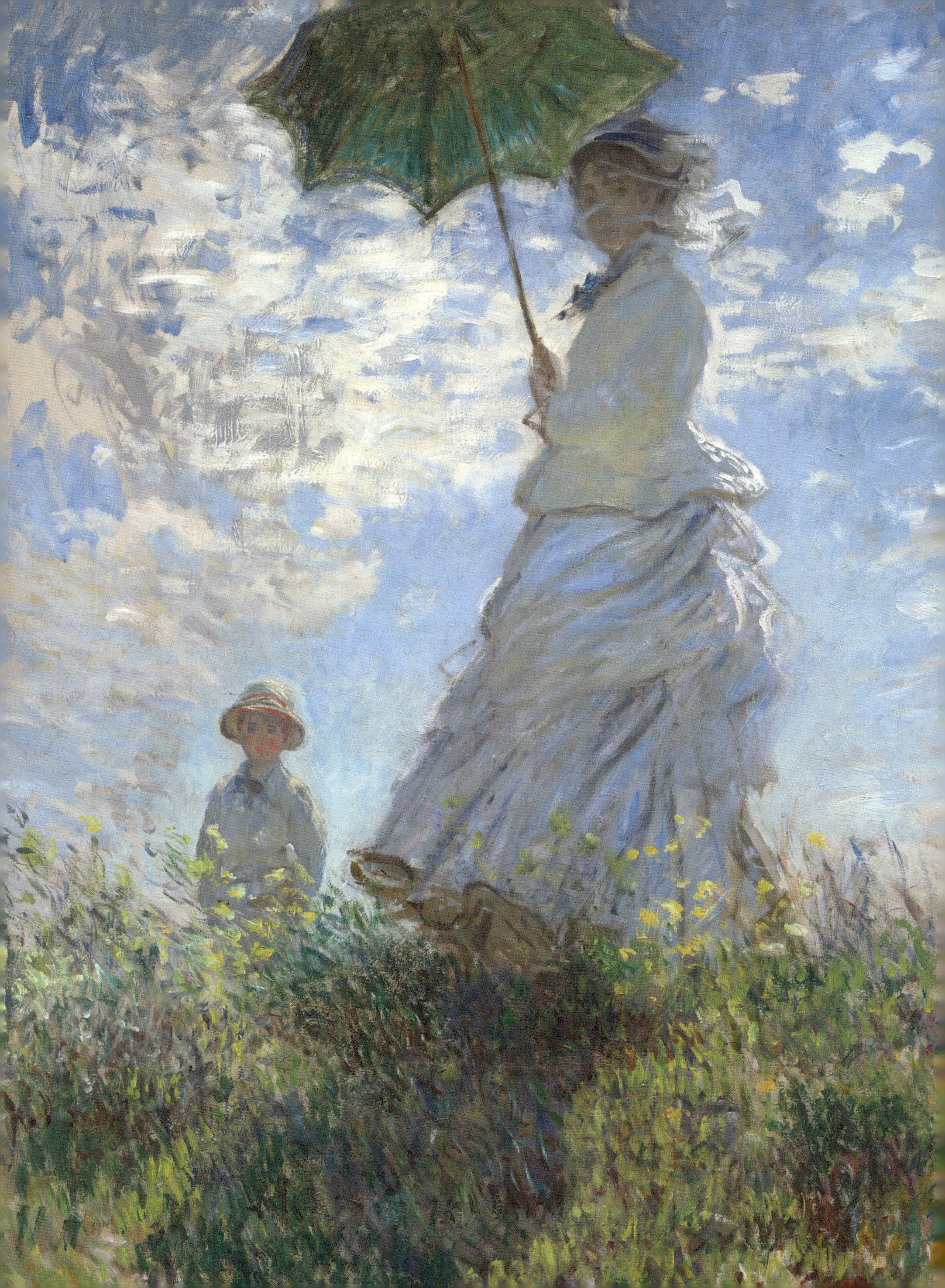

'Children Playing on the Beach'

Mary Cassatt, 1884

National Gallery of Art

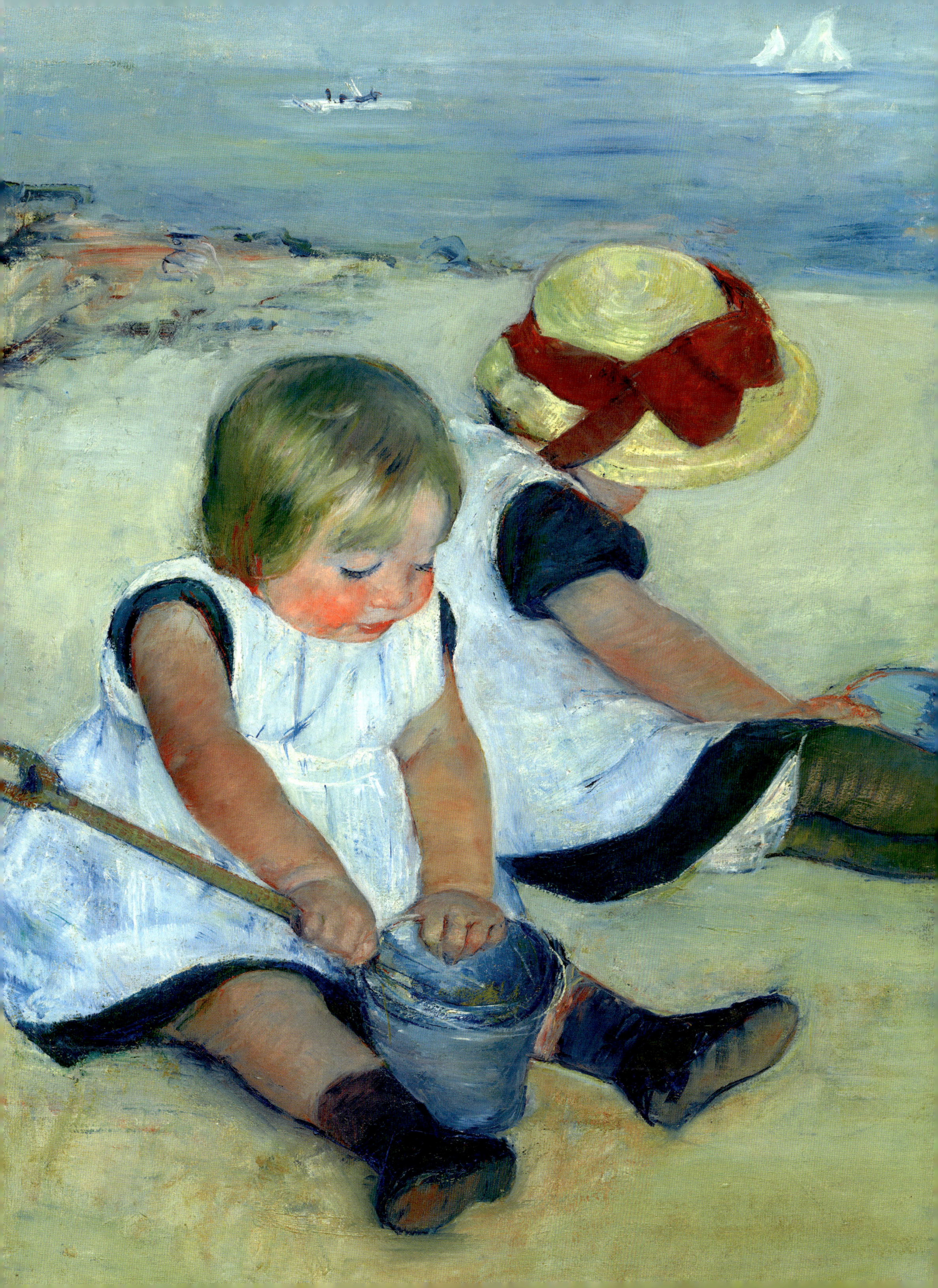

'By the seashore'
Auguste Renoir, 1884

Metropolitan Museum of Art

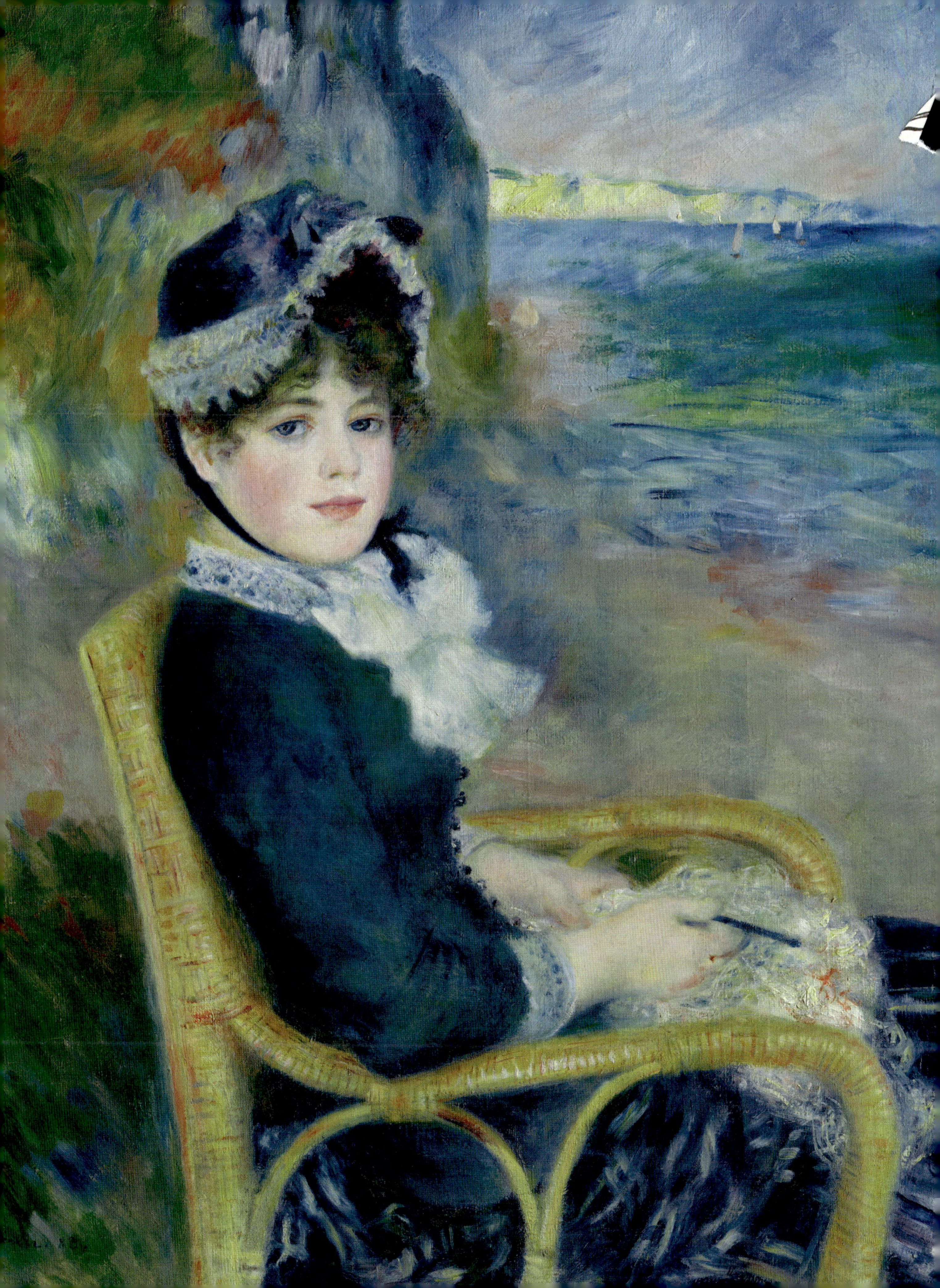

'The Boating Party'

Mary Cassatt, 1894

National Gallery of Art

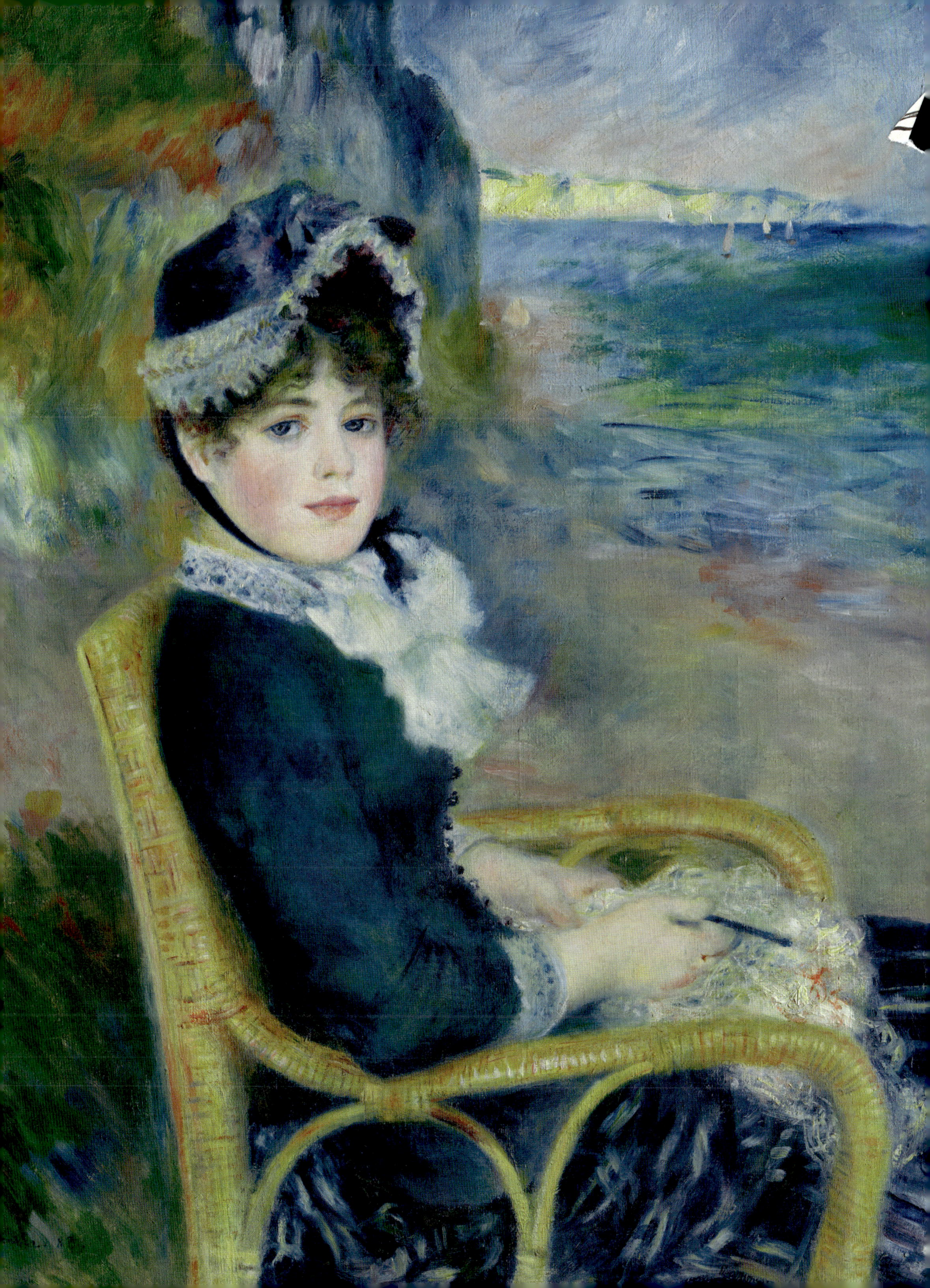

'The Boating Party'

Mary Cassatt, 1894

National Gallery of Art

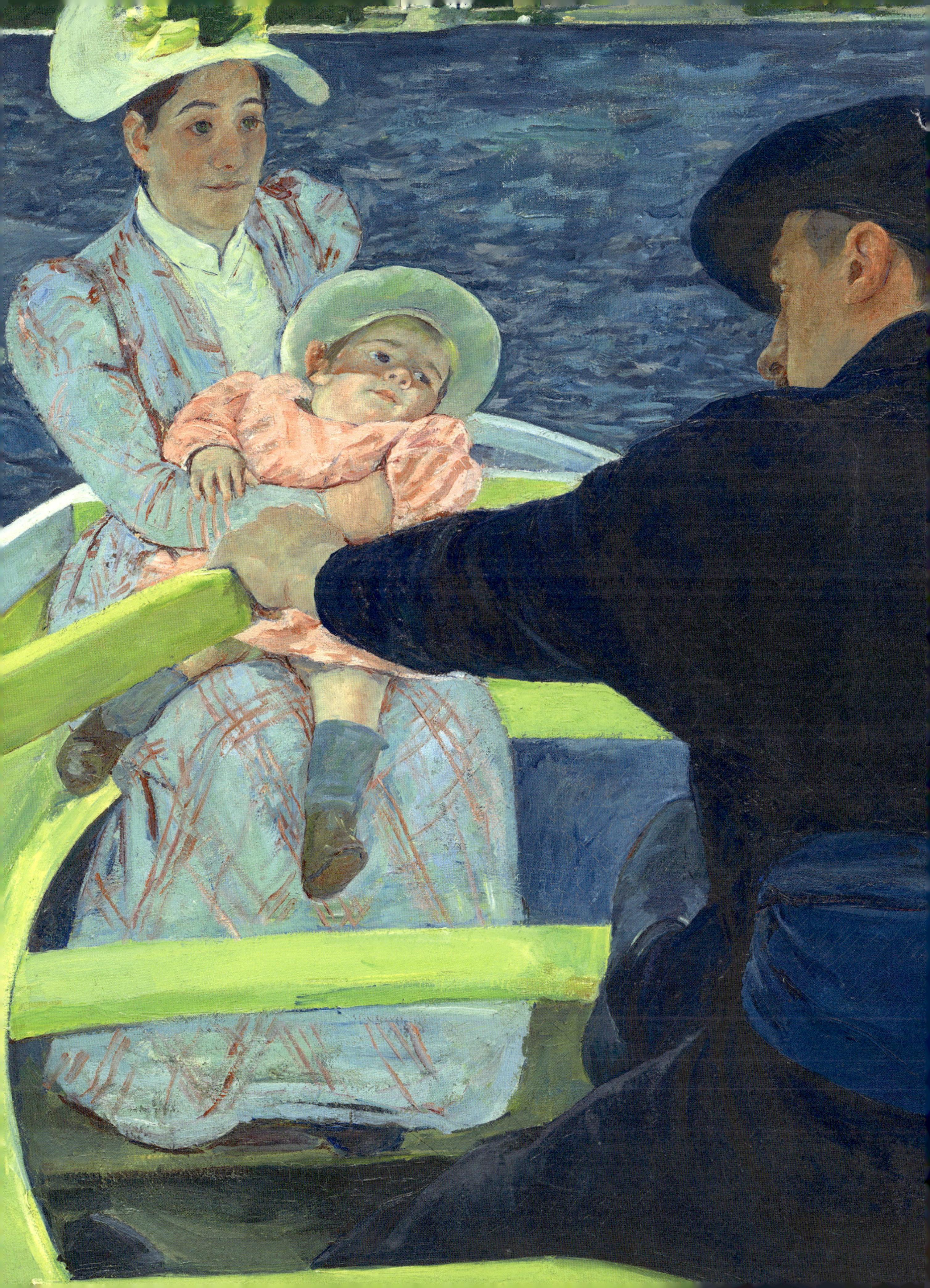

'Arrival of the Normandy train, Gare Saint Lazare'
Claude Monet, 1887

Art Institute of Chicago

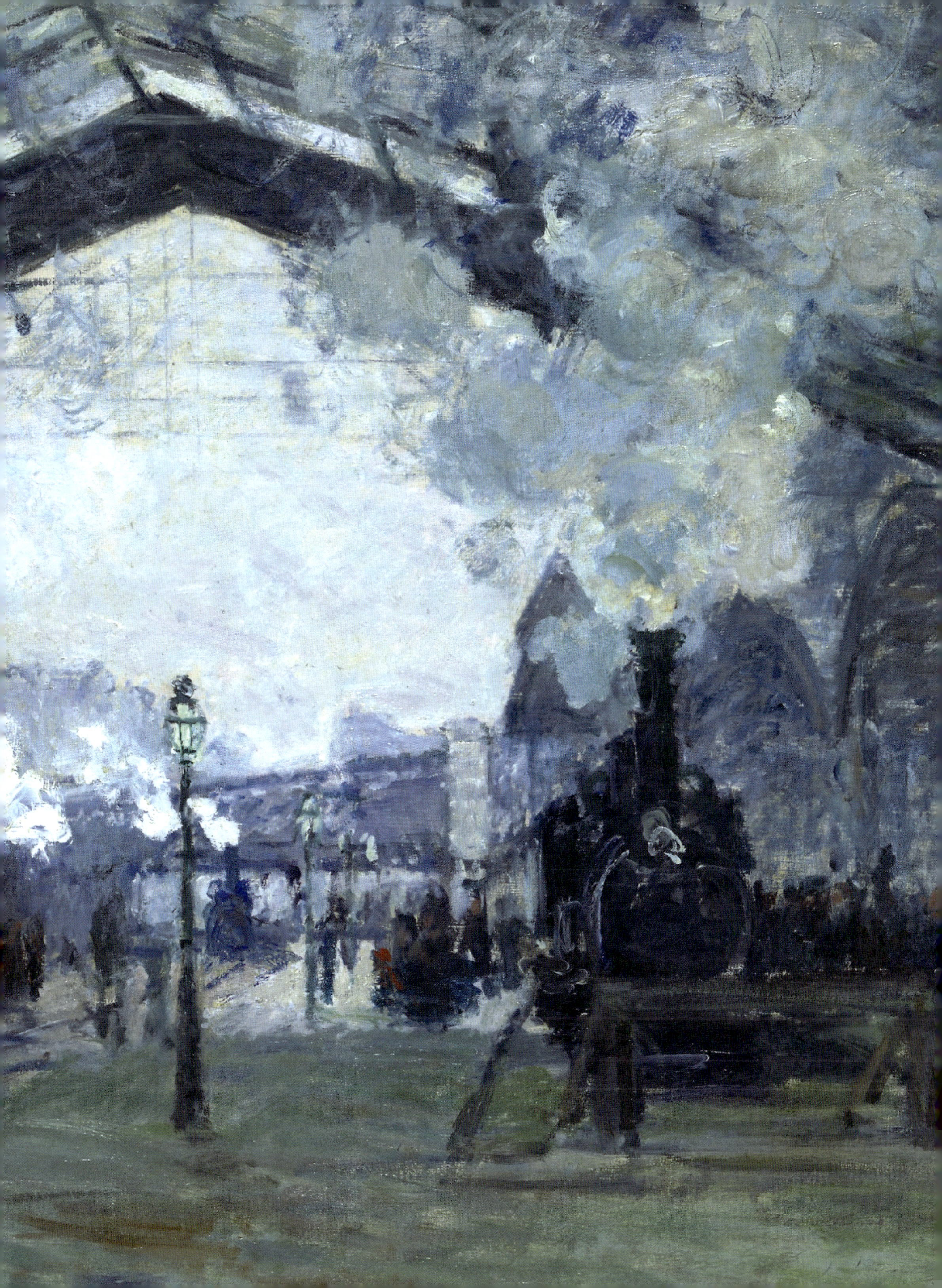

'Ships Riding on the Seine at Rouen'

Claude Monet, 1873

National Gallery of Art

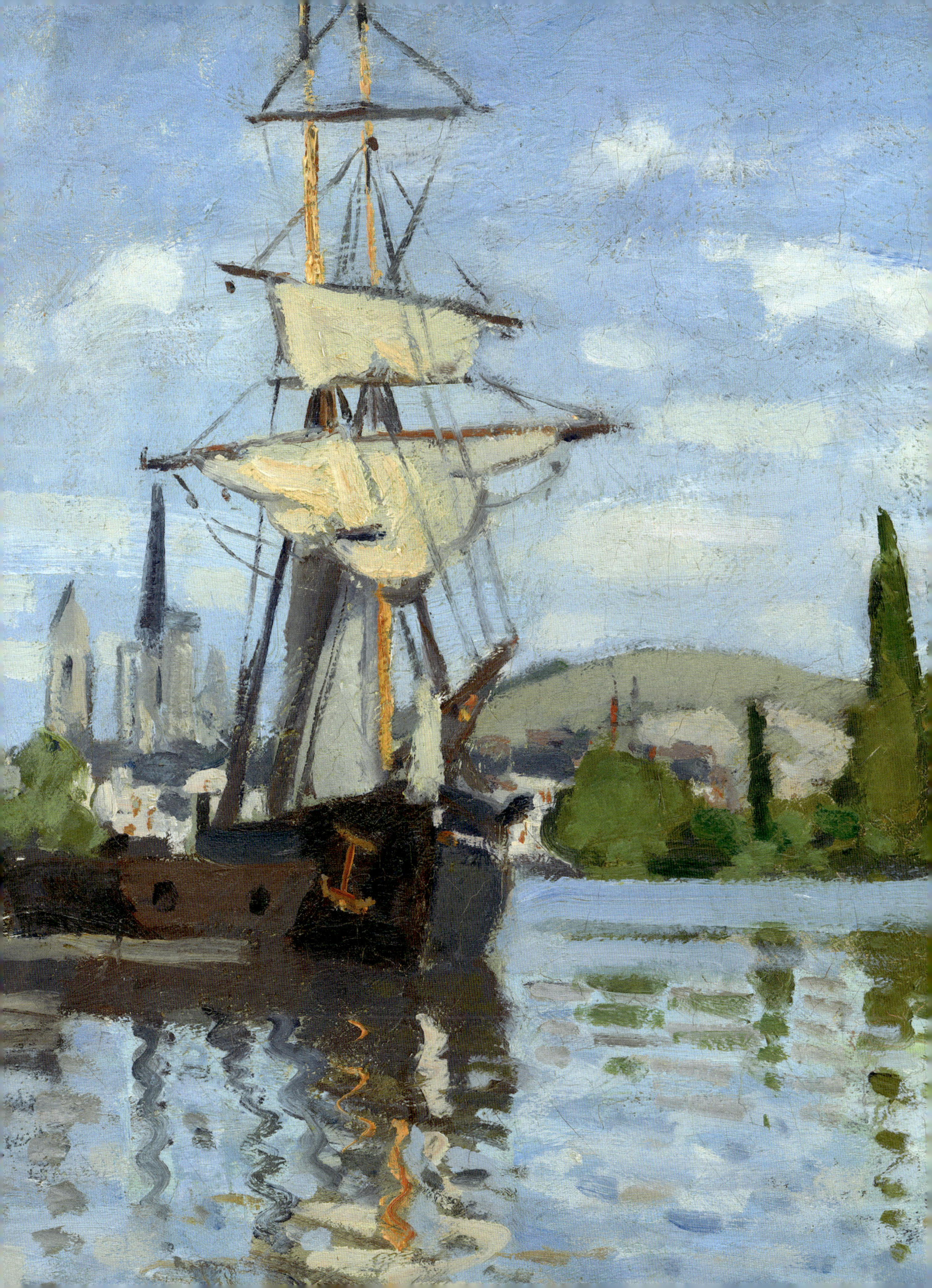

'The Laundress'

Honore Daumier, 1863

Metropolitan Museum of Art

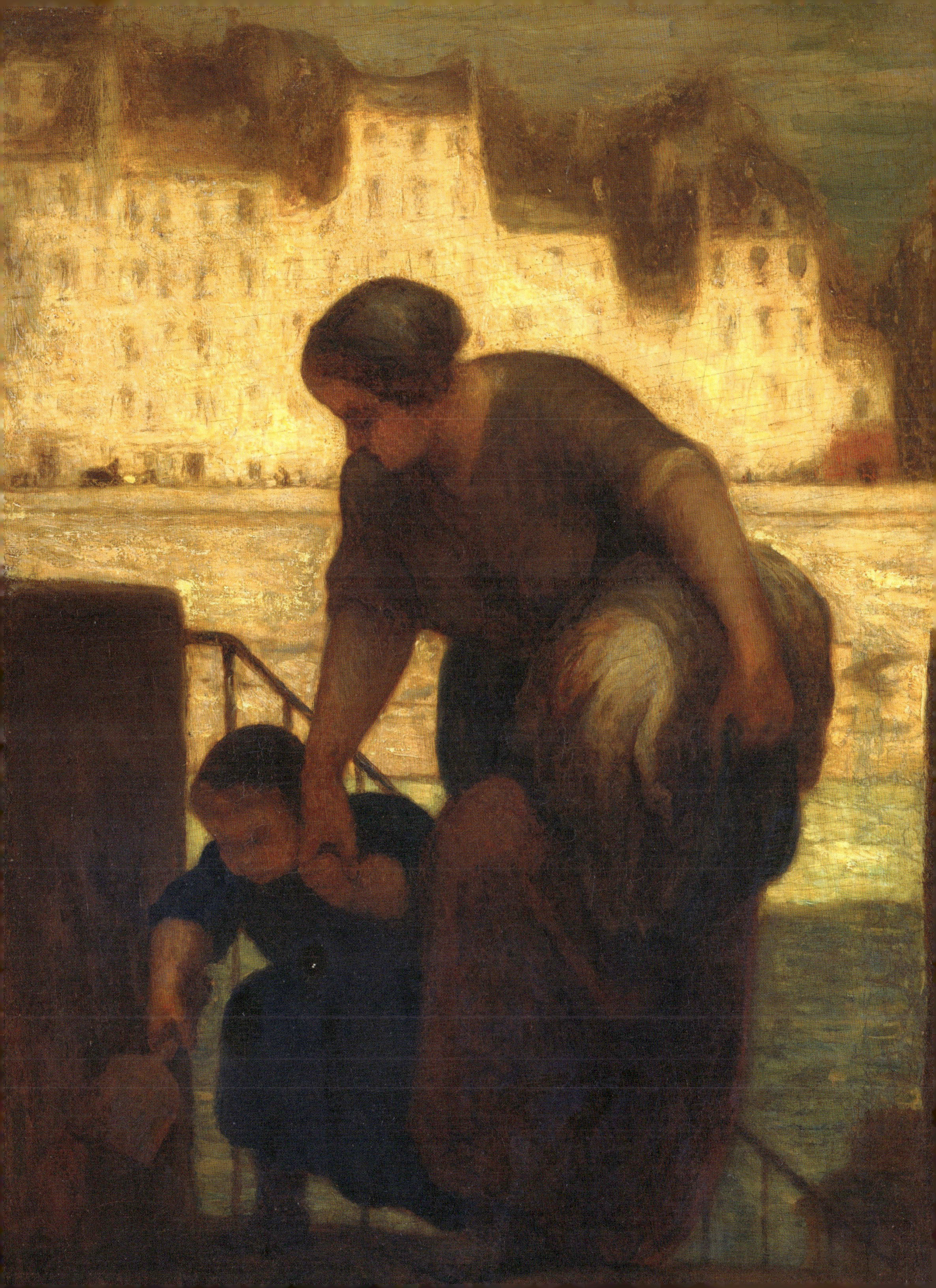

'Breton Girls Dancing, Port Aven'

Paul Gauguin, 1888

National Gallery of Art

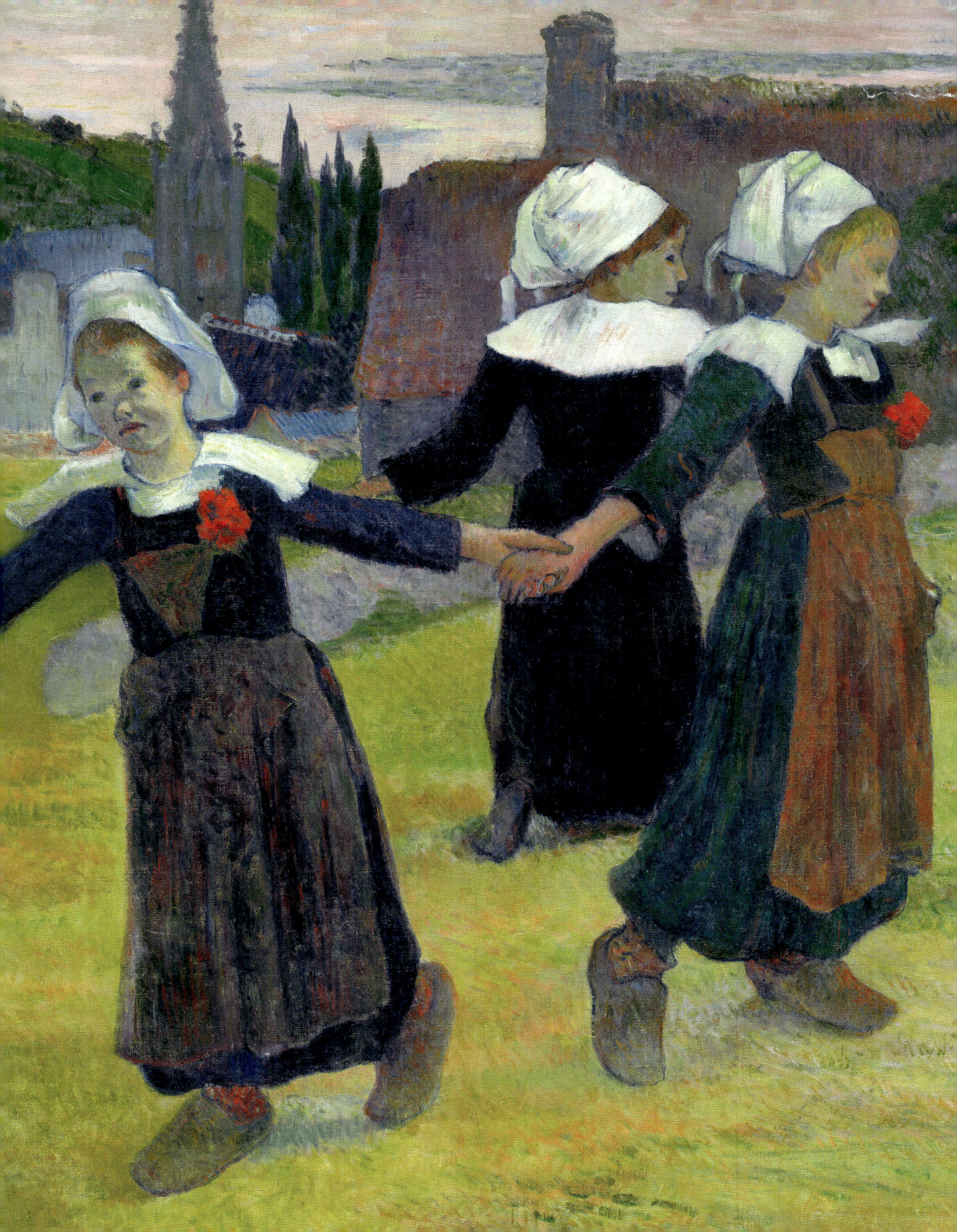

'On A Balcony'

Mary Cassatt, 1879

Art Institute of Chicago

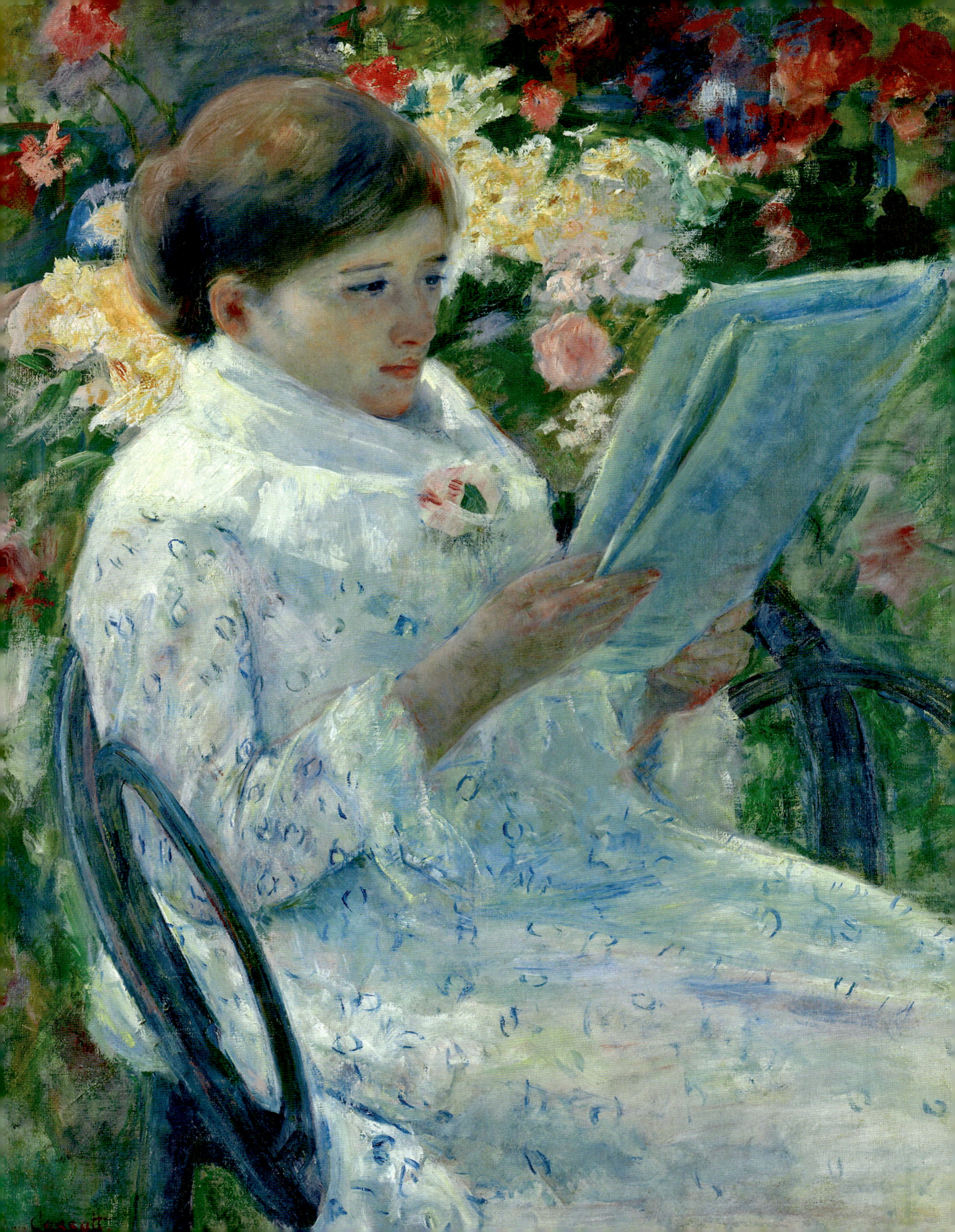

'The House with the Cracked Walls'

Paul Cezanne, 1894

Metropolitan Museum of Art

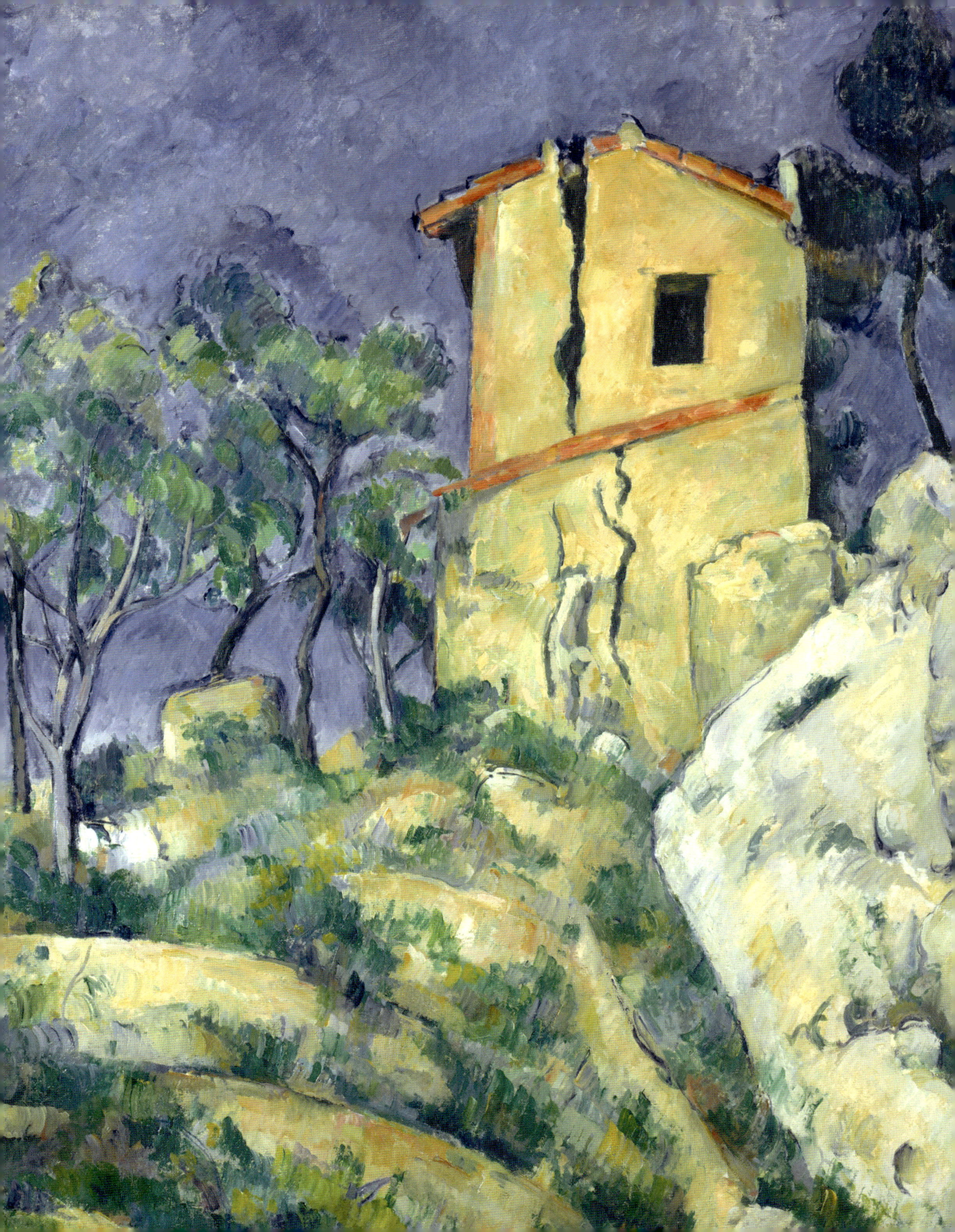

'Wheat Fields and The Cypresses'
Vincent van Gogh, 1883

Metropolitan Museum of Art

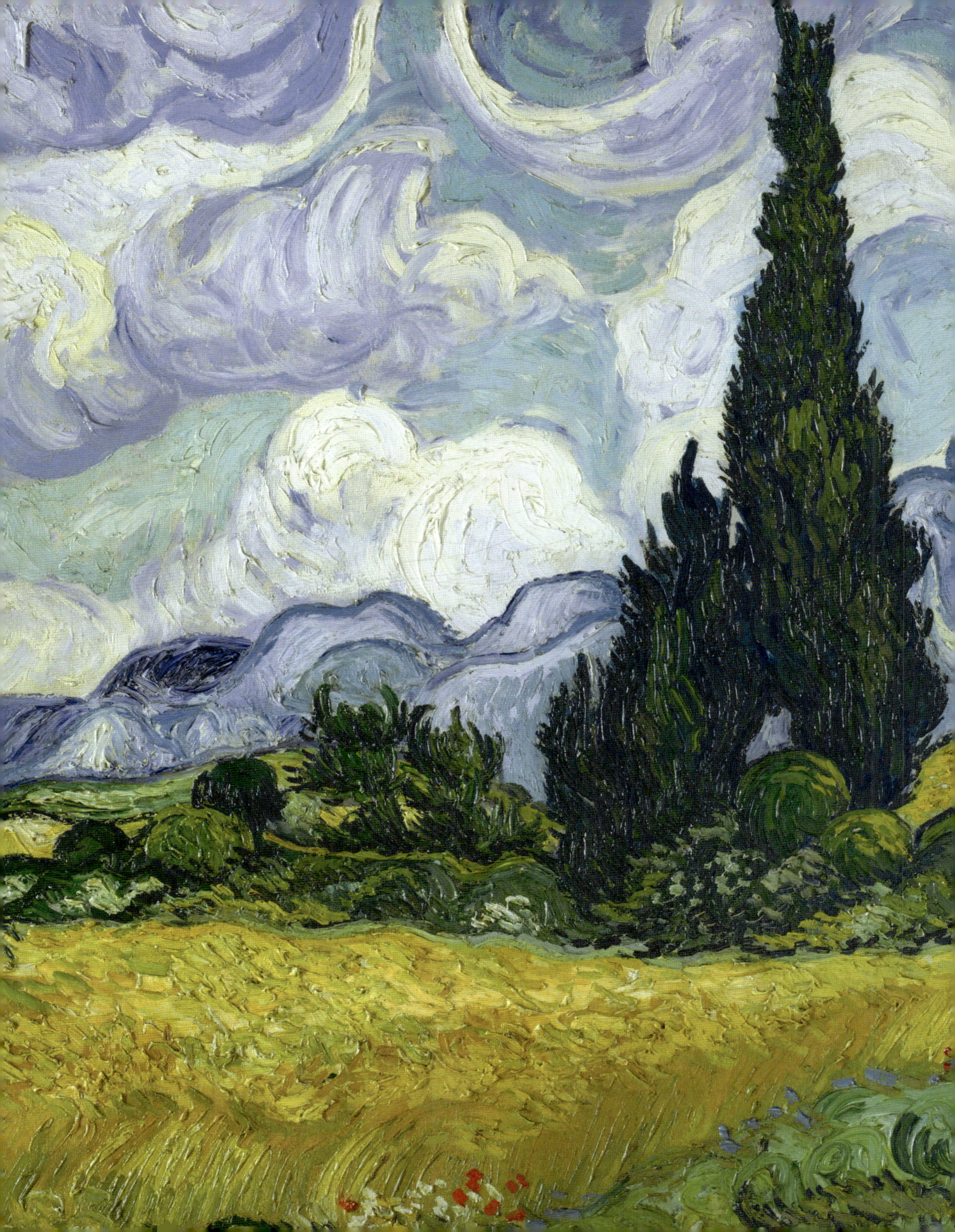

'Haystacks in Brittany'

Paul Gauguin, 1890

National Gallery of Art

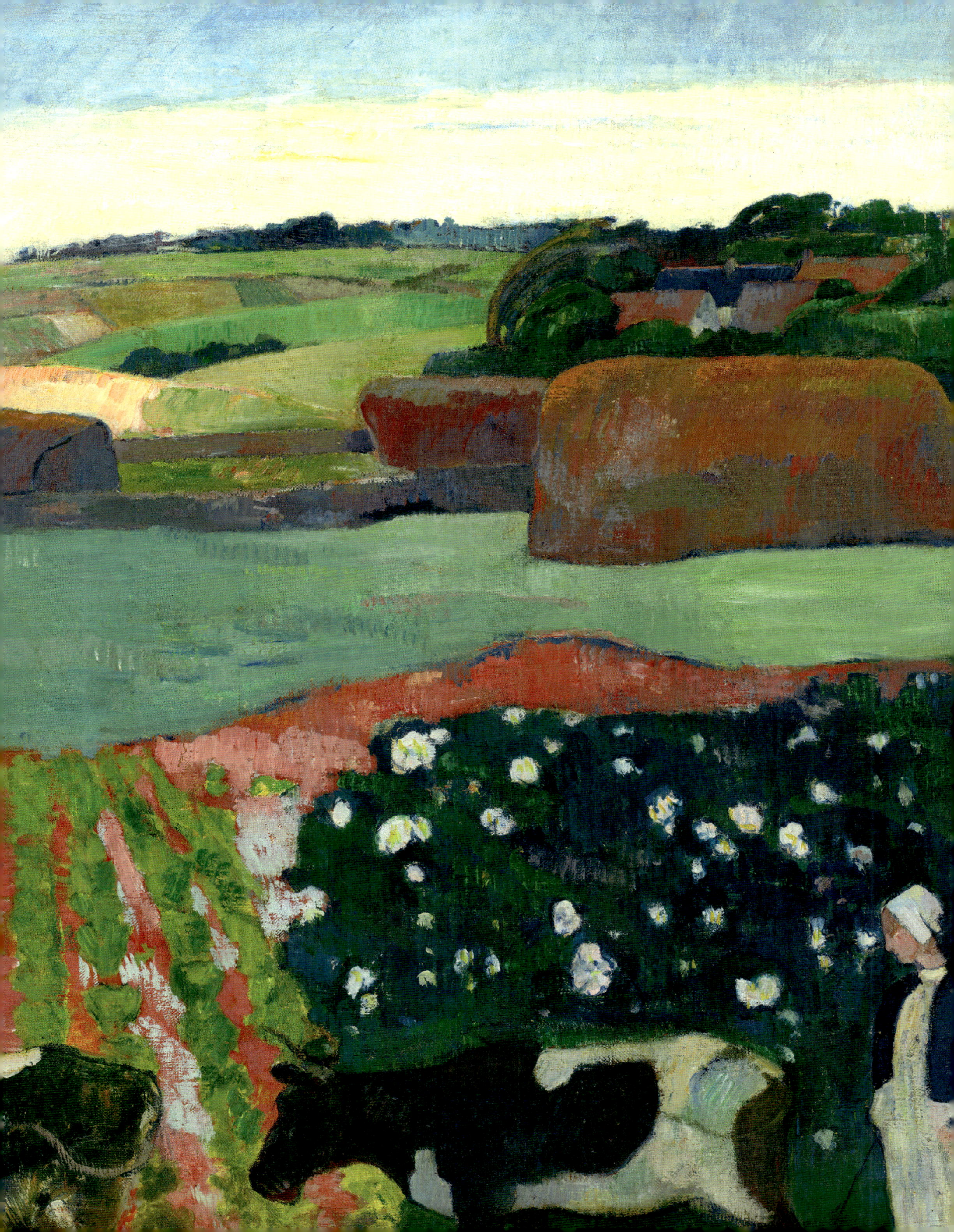

'The Harvest, Pontoise'

Camille Pissarro, 1881

Metropolitan Museum of Art

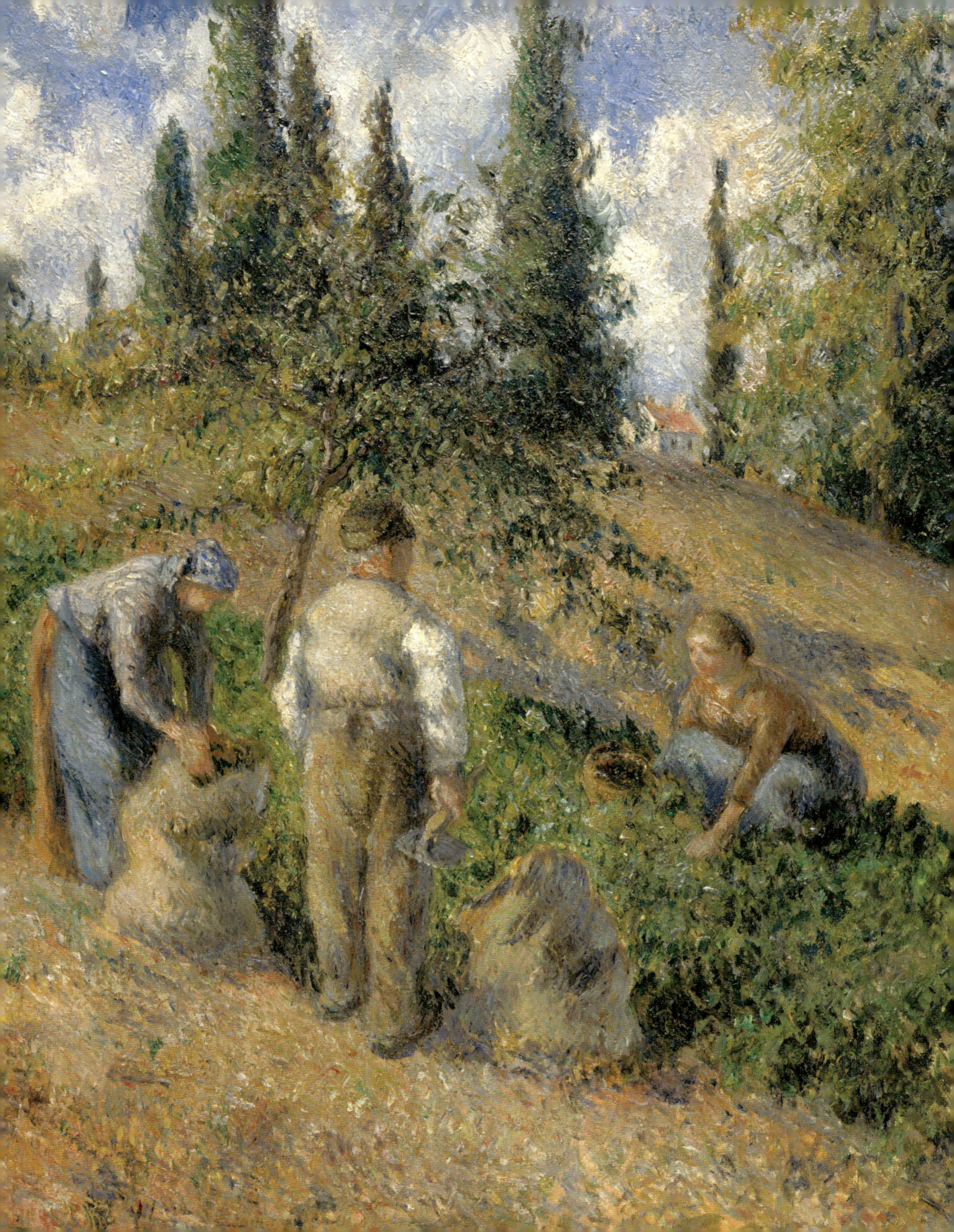

'Snap the Whip'

Winslow Homer, 1872

Metropolitan Museum of Art

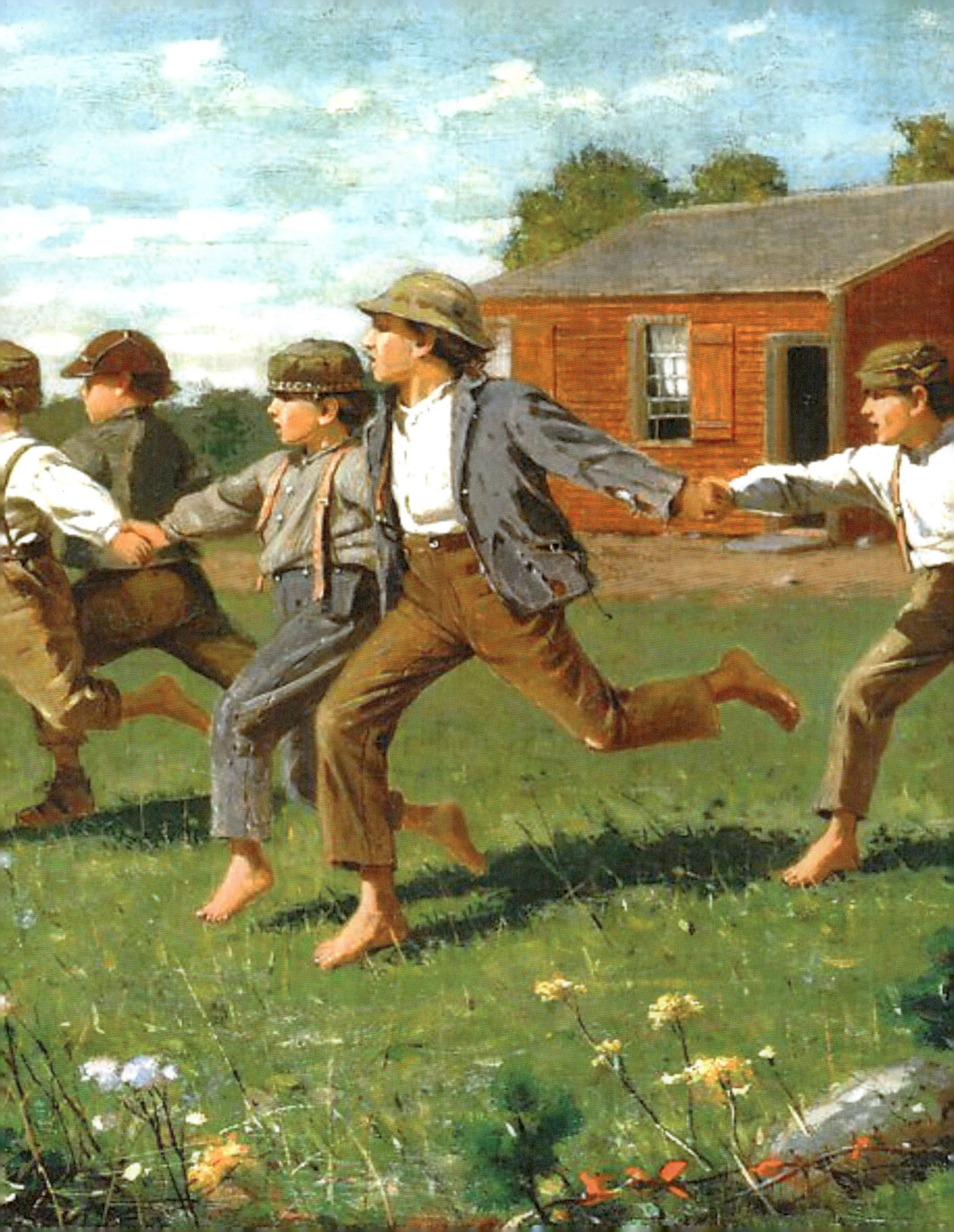

'The Dance Class'
Edgar Degas, 1874

Metropolitan Museum of Art

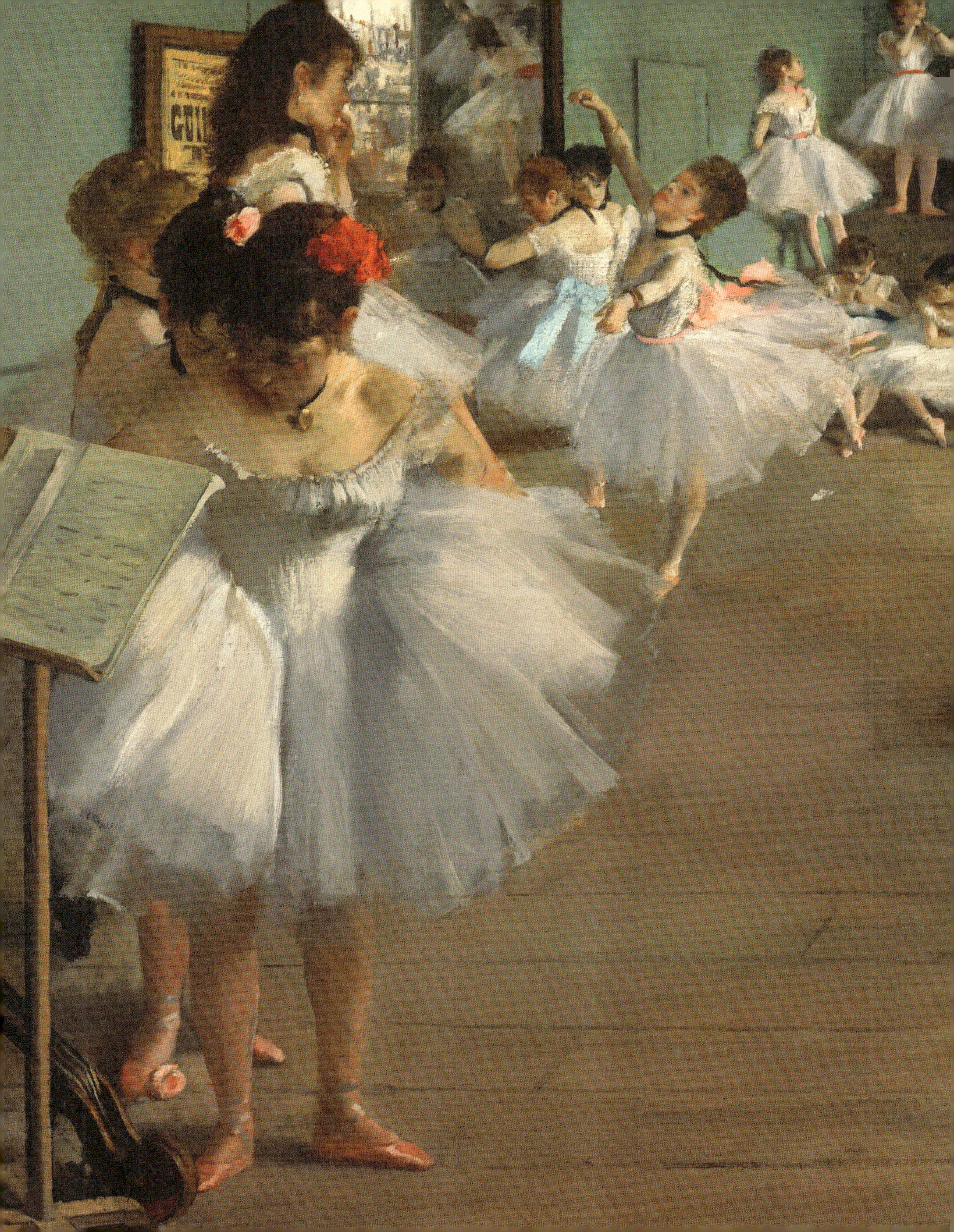

'Two Young Girls at the Piano'
Auguste Renoir, 1892

Metropolitan Museum of Art

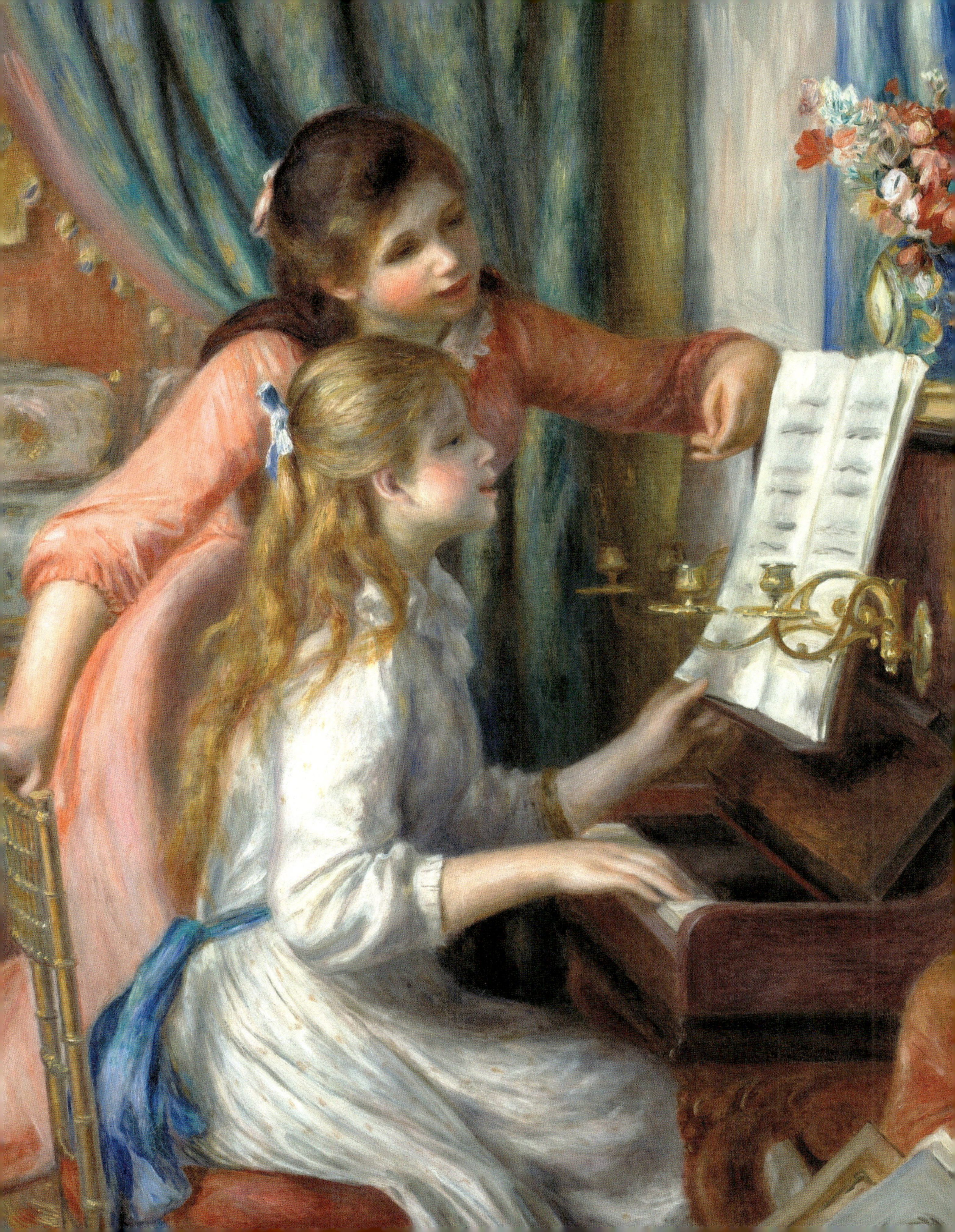

'Jean Renoir Sewing'

Auguste Renoir, 1899

Art Institute of Chicago

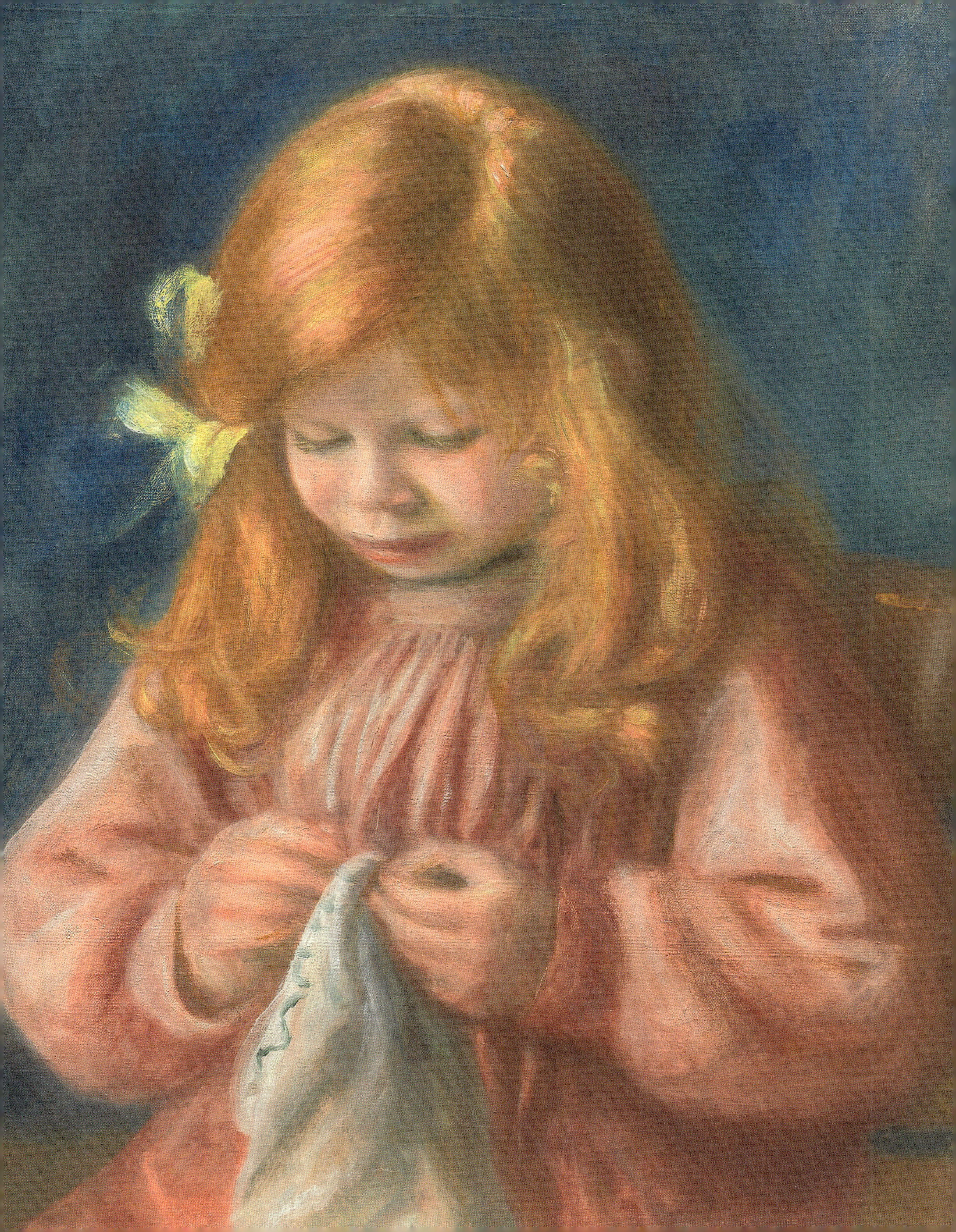

'Roses'
Vincent van Gogh, 1890

Metropolitan Museum of Art

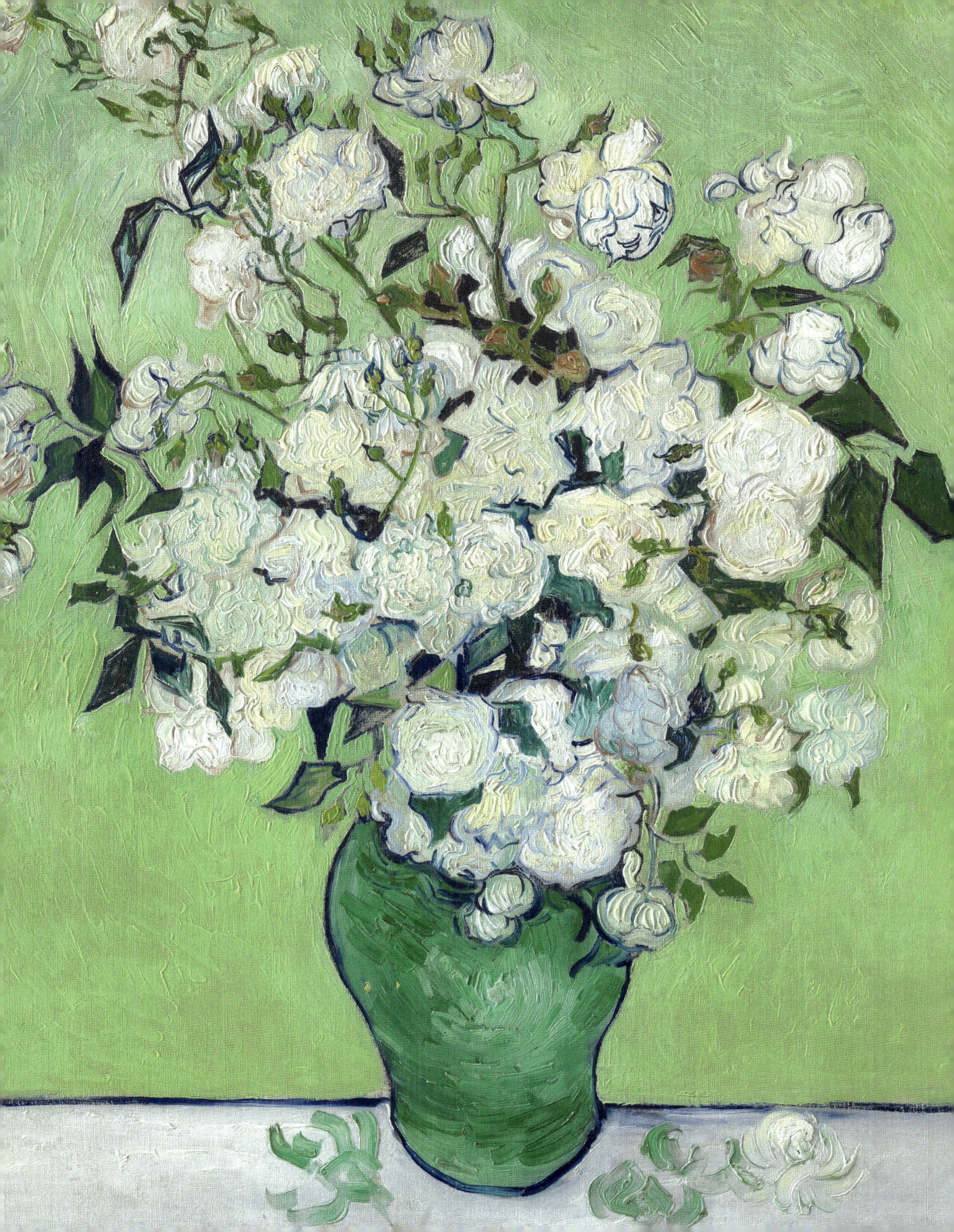

'Two Sisters (On The Terrace)'

Auguste Renoir, 1881

Art Institute of Chicago

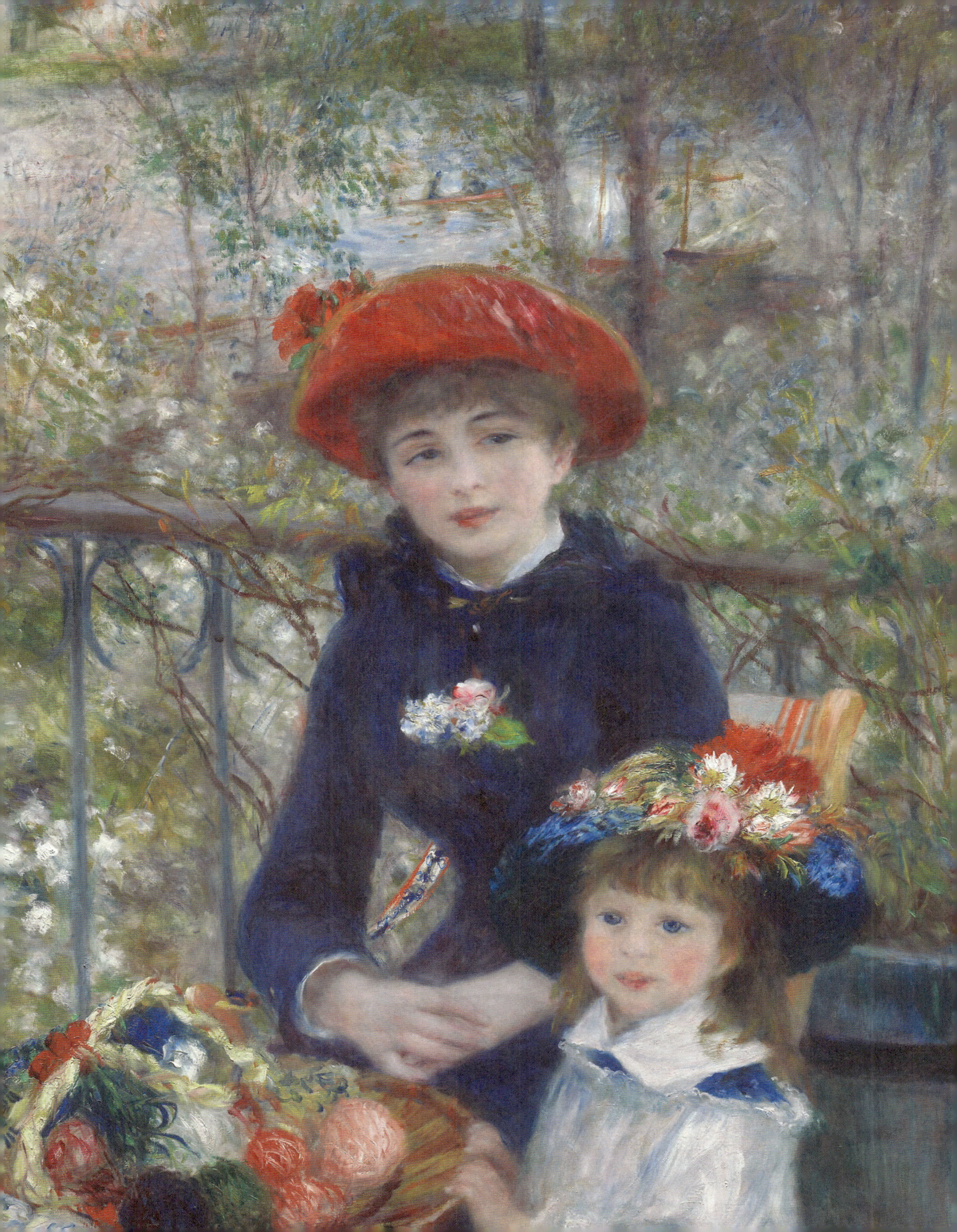

'Rabbits on a Log'

Arthur Fitzwilliam Tait, 1897

Metropolitan Museum of Art

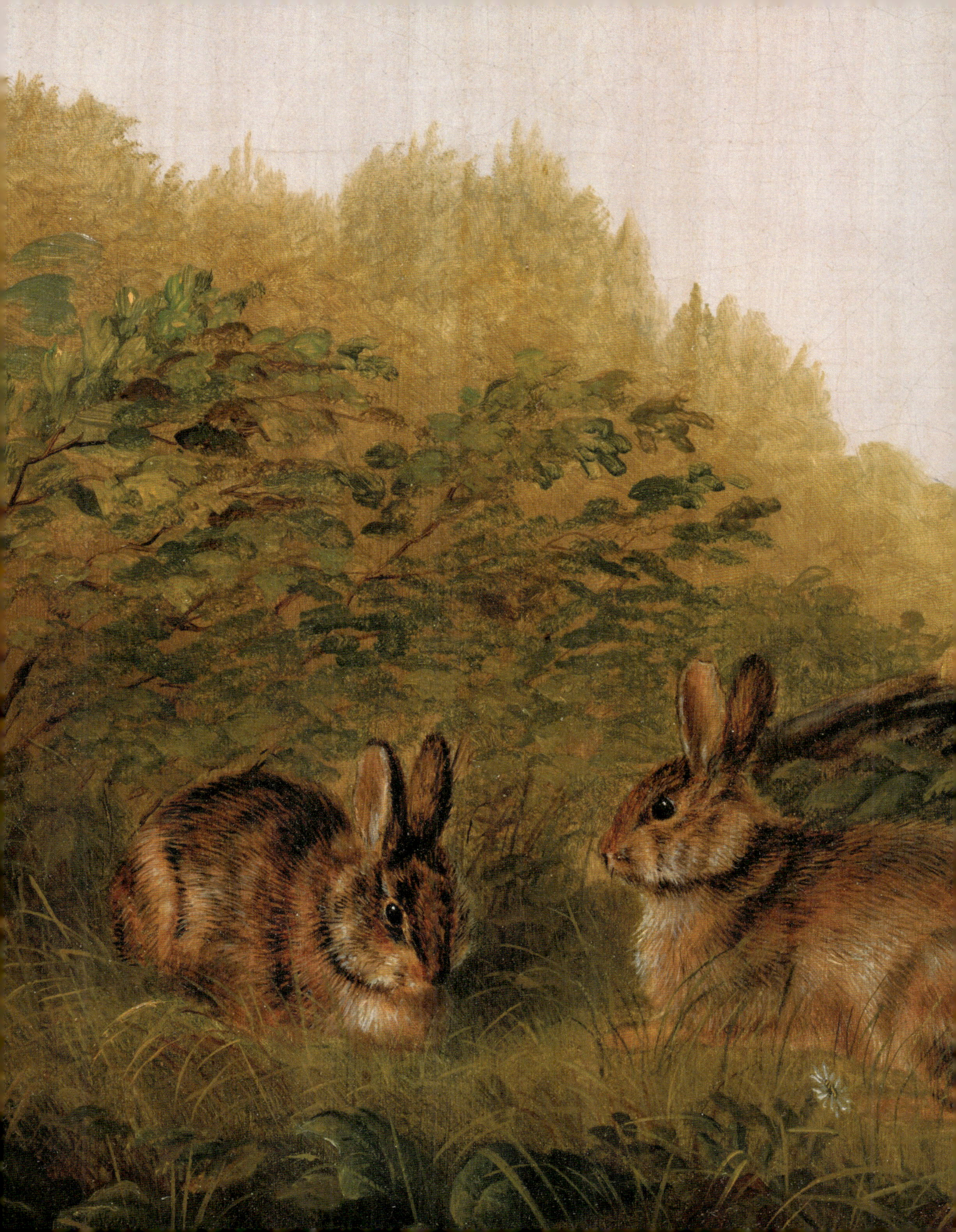

'At the Seaside'
William Merritt Chase, 1892

Metropolitan Museum of Art

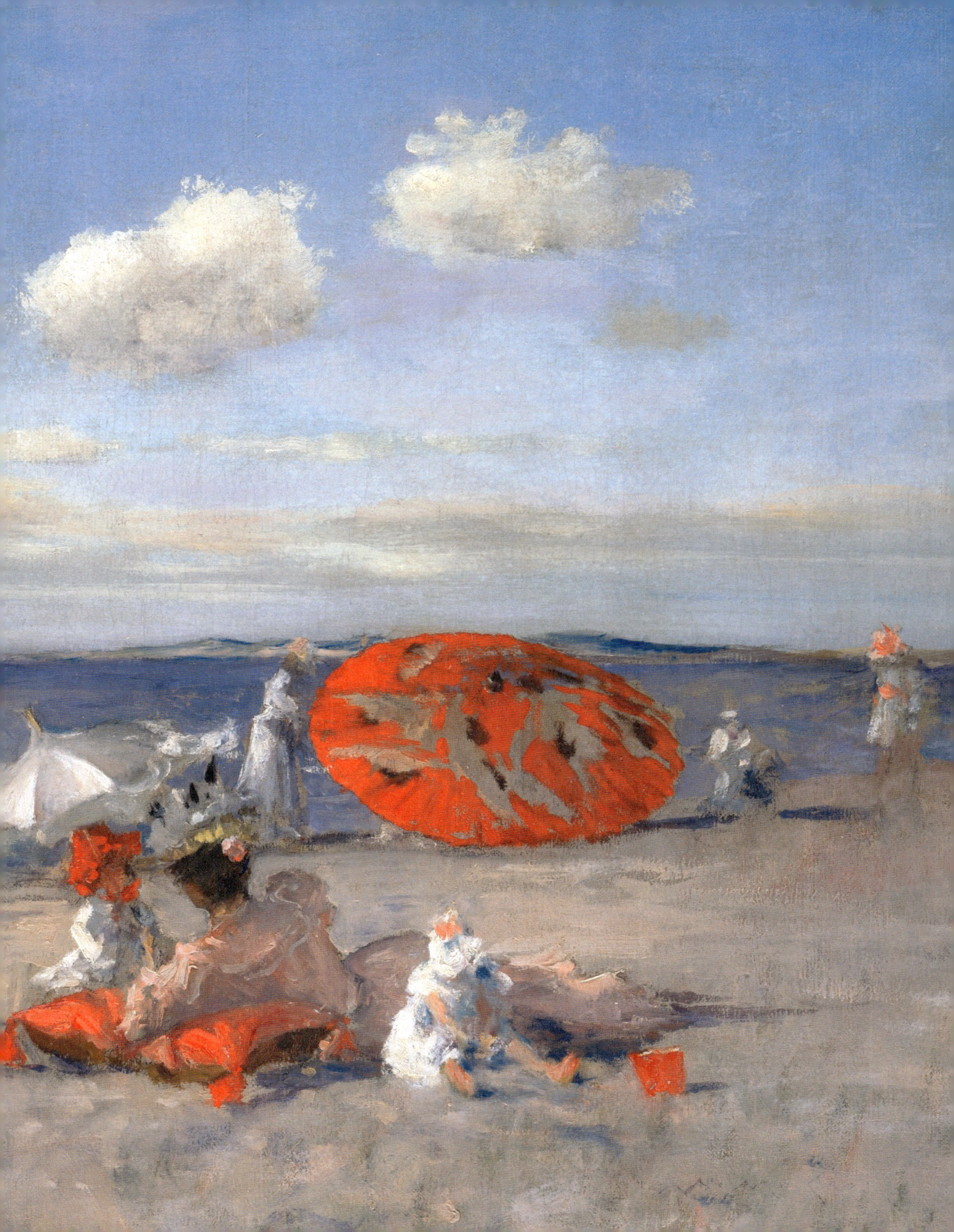

'Figures on the Beach'

Auguste Renoir, 1890

Metropolitan Museum of Art

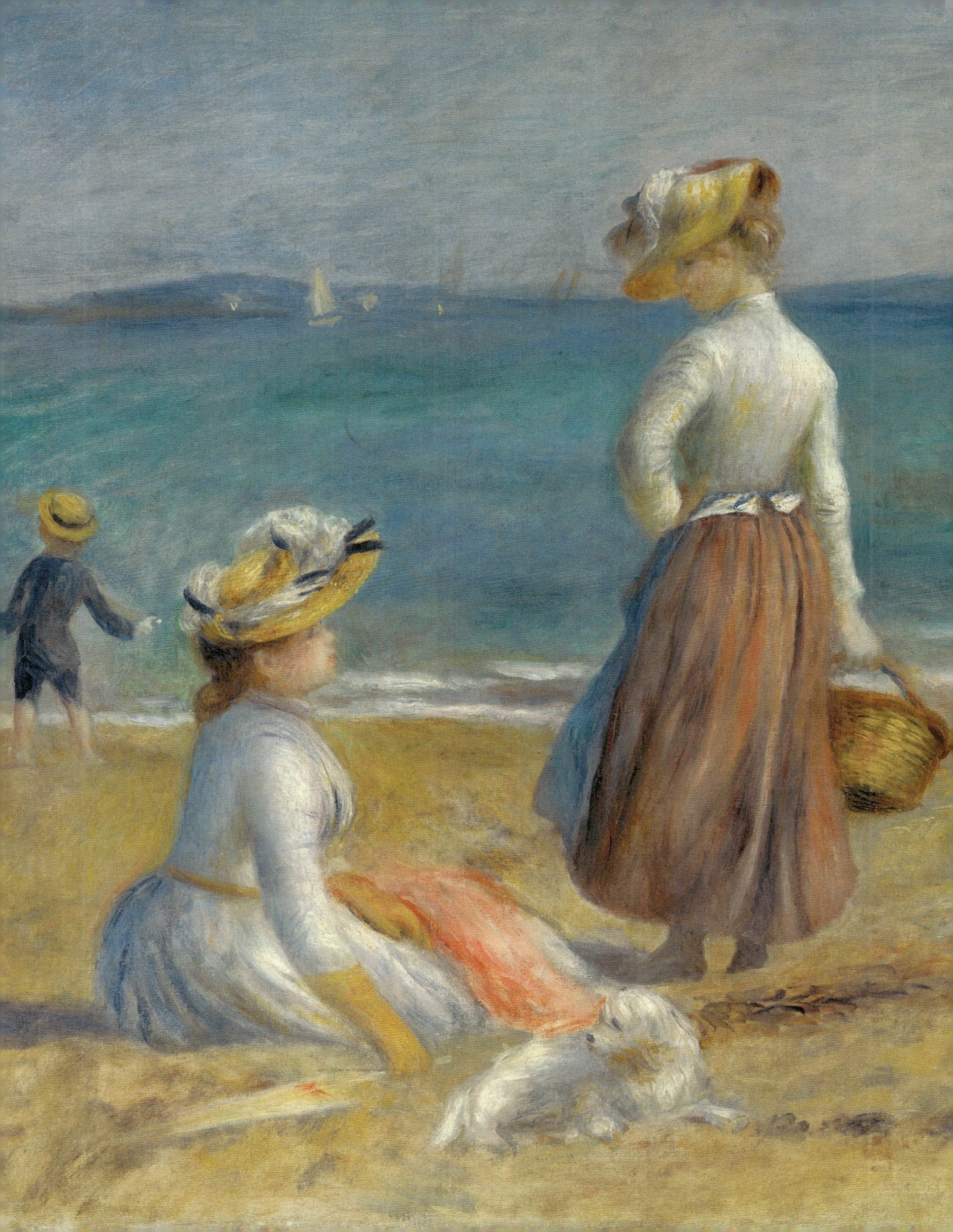

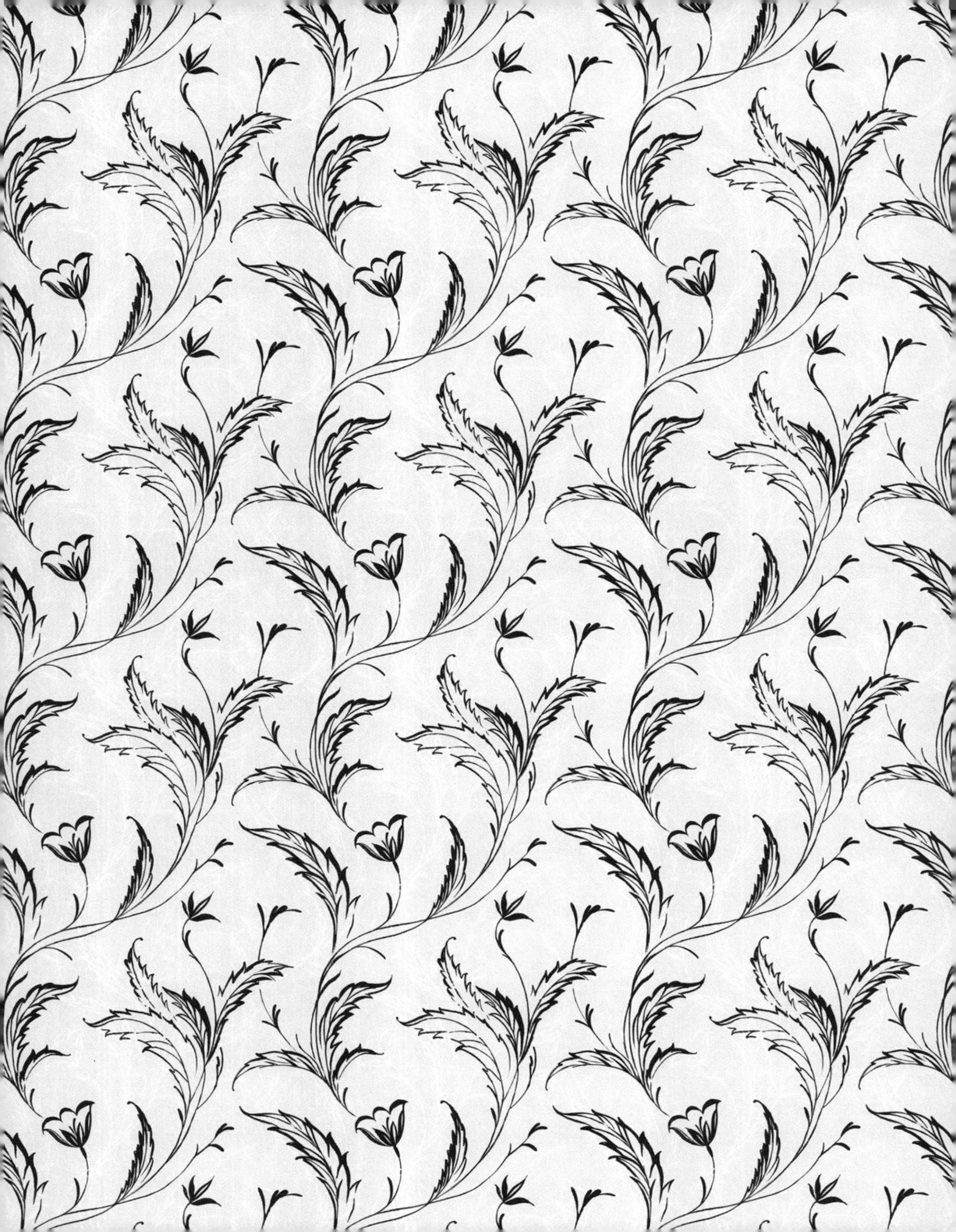

Printed in Great Britain
by Amazon